Family:

It's All Relative

Patricia K. JuAire

DORRANCE
PUBLISHING CO
EST. 1920
PITTSBURGH, PENNSYLVANIA 15238

Dorrance Publishing Co
585 Alpha Drive
Suite 103
Pittsburgh, PA 15238
Visit our website at *www.dorrancebookstore.com*

ISBN: 978-1-6393-7239-3
eISBN: 978-1-6393-7641-4

Family:

It's All Relative

This manuscript is dedicated to my parents:
Roberta Lynn McPurdy (Bronson, Ostrander, Jarrett, Drake) aka
Bert—who taught me a number of valuable lessons about being a
mother.
Susie Taylor Johnson - who taught me the difference between a
mother and a mom.
Wayne Daniel Bronson aka Goose - who taught me valuable lessons
about being a father.
Richard Dean Ostrander aka Dick - who taught me the difference
between a father and a dad.
And to my senior English teacher and mentor
Gloria Graham Flynn aka Glo—who, at a dinner where she was the
keynote speaker, said she was waiting for me to write my book. I don't
know if this is what she had in mind, but here it is.

The following definitions were located at www.merriamwebster.com.

family (n): the basic unit in society traditionally consisting of two parents rearing their children; also: any of various social units differing from but regarded as equivalent to the traditional family.

relative (n): a person connected by blood or affinity with another

relative (adj): relevant or pertinent

"Family isn't about whose blood you have. It's about who you care about." - Trey Parker & Matt Stone, South Park, Ep. "Ike's Wee Wee," 1998.

1   Summer 1998: I was a thirty-one-year-old wife with an eight-year-old daughter and a six-year-old son. We were the "traditional" family living the American Dream, minus the dog and the picket fence.

2   Two years later, I was a thirty-three-year-old widow with a ten-year-old daughter, an eight-year-old son, and no idea how to help my family of only three now keep it together, let alone move forward.

3   Twenty-one more years later, I found myself reflecting on how I got here, trying to figure out how to be the new matriarch, which led me to wonder what that even means: FAMILY.

4   The problem with memories is how much is actual memory and how much is what we think we remember based on pictures and/or stories; reality or perception?

5   This is what I think I know about my family. Some is absolute fact and can be proven; some is my perception.

It was March 1967. My mother had turned eighteen in September of 1966; my father had turned twenty-four (I think) in October of 1966. They already had a daughter who was born in November of 1965. She was planned; I was not. The marriage was an agreement of sorts not a love match. My mother wanted away from her mother and stepfather, and my father was okay with marriage and a child. From pictures, we looked acceptably happy; there were no family photos of the four of us, though.

An accident with a fireplace left my mother with some time in the hospital and minor scars on her legs. It left me with months in a burn center almost two hours from home, numerous surgeries and hospital stays over the next twelve to fifteen years, and quite a bit of scarring on my arms, legs, and torso with a couple of scars on my ass. Less than a year after the accident, my biological parents divorced. I never really heard why. My father was given custody of my only full sibling and I. We stayed with his parents for a few months before he remarried; all of a sudden, I had a new family; I was four.

Flashes of memories from this time period pop through my mind in a jumble with no real fluidity or appreciation of time. We were a family of four for four years until they had a daughter—my half-sister. I don't have any memories from these years that are pleasant. My mother once told me she thinks things were okay for a year or so, but then my father and stepmother began drinking heavily based on what she heard and saw during visitations. What I remember most is fear. And trauma.

We're led to believe that parents, especially, but family in general, love and care for one another. That was not my experience in this household. I remember being forced to sit at the table, forced to eat until I threw up, at which time I was yelled at for wasting food then sent to bed. I remember my older sister eating brownies before school and lying about it after school, resulting in both of us being whipped repeatedly until a confession was made. I remember receiving another whipping for lying when I said it was me in order to stop the original punishment. I remember irritating my father once to the point that he grabbed me by the hair and threw me across the room without letting go. I doubt the resulting patch of missing hair was easy to explain. I remember we told them we wanted to live with our mother one winter. Permission was granted with the caveat that the only items we could take with us were things our mother had given us.

I should point out that our paternal grandmother made the majority of our clothes, so our mother didn't purchase clothing items for us. As a result, we left for the two-mile trip to town, snow on the ground, each carrying a sack of toys in our arms, wearing only underpants. With no concept of time, I don't know how long we were outside walking. I do know our stepmother picked us up in the car when we were about a quarter of a mile from town. I remember another time when we were awakened in the middle of the night before being thrown outside to sleep because we had eaten more than four slices of bread (two each was the limit).

Somewhere in the midst of all of that and more, my mother remarried. This man, her second husband, would become my dad and remain so after they divorced, after they both remarried yet again, until his death a few months ago.

My full sister and I spent our visitation weekends with one of my mother's brothers who lived about fifteen miles away and had kids around the same ages. This set of uncle, aunt, and cousins gave me a clue that my "family" wasn't the same as other people's. The first time my sister and I ran away from our father's house, we got on the bus with our cousins after school. This was also my first run-in with the police since the sheriff's department came to retrieve us. I learned several years later that my uncle and aunt were almost arrested when they initially refused to let us leave because of bruises we had from being beaten with boards by our father and stepmother.

Another run away expedition found us at the business where our mother and stepfather worked. A trip to the local welfare office (NKA

DCF), a trial, and an unknown amount of time later, my "family" changed again when our mother was granted residential custody. Within three or four years at most, my mother made the decision to place her oldest daughter into state custody for a number of reasons that aren't really part of this story, except to say that my mother cut one child loose to ensure the safety of the other.

Having been forced to call my stepmother "Mom" from the day she married my father, I expected a similar forced edict when I moved in with my mother. That was not the case; I was given the option of using my stepfather's name, his nickname, or Dad if I wanted to. I don't know how long it took, but he soon became Dad.

I had to take a break from this manuscript for a few weeks; as cathartic as this can be, it can also be overwhelming as the trauma is experienced again through the words.

I'm not sure when it came to my unconscious attention that my mother wasn't really cut out to be a mom ... I know I was over thirty when I accepted and understood that she did the best she could; she just wasn't very good at it. Don't get me wrong, there were moments here and there, but in the grand scheme of things, it was not her forte.

The first thing I remember that felt "motherly," so to speak, was when she did something unheard of at the time (and rare even now) by signing custody of her oldest child over to the State of Kansas out of fear for my safety. Technically, that would have been the second motherly decision. When my biological parents divorced, she gave custody to my father because he was older and had a stable job; at the time, he was the better parent, and she knew it.

There's a gap in there between saving my eleven- to twelve-year-old self from the unstable clutches of an older sister and the next "motherly" event. During the gap, several memories of not so motherly stuff were taking up space. Let me be clear, this was long before any type of child abuse was considered bad parenting let alone verbal or emotional child abuse. Both of my biological parents and my stepmother would be arrested in a heartbeat in the twenty-first century.

Somewhere around twelve or thirteen, maybe fourteen, I forgot to water the dogs one summer day. In order to ensure I never forgot again, my mother chained me to the propane tank all day without water. She made her point; I make sure the animals are taken care of first. Of course, it could also play into why I don't have pets often....

At thirteen, I spent the summer with her best friend after she had surgery. This was the first time I spent an extended length of time with someone other than family. It was the best summer; I didn't get yelled at or belittled or degraded. I felt like an actual person and appreciated by others.

At fifteen or so, when most of my friends were getting some type of birds and bees talk from their parents, I received a more direct approach from my mother while we were cleaning stalls. To paraphrase as I remember it: Mother, "I suppose you'll be thinking about having sex at some point. You should know it isn't all it's cracked up to be; the first time is never any good; and I'm too young to be a grandmother, so do without it for as long as you can. When you can't, tell me and we'll go to the doctor's office." I don't recall saying anything in response. She never stopped shoveling manure and straw as she said any of it; it was surreal.

At about the same time, she pulled off motherly event number two. I had a check-up with my plastic surgeon to check my burn scars and growth to determine if more grafts were necessary. I was becoming interested in boys, and friends were starting to date. I wasn't being asked out by anyone, and I was convinced it was because I was ugly with all the scars. At some point, I expressed these thoughts to my mother. Her pearl of wisdom this time was just as succinct but not surreal. She said, "If someone can't see past some scars, why would you want to go out with them or even be friends with them? Those kinds of people are shallow and won't stick when you need them the most." The rearview mirror has proved that to be rock solid advice and completely true.

Of course, like all lightning bolts, it flashed its brilliance and was over in a minute. I was sixteen the year I qualified for the state finals in barrel racing. I was so excited, and I thought that surely my mother would finally have something about me to be proud of. I was wrong. The competition was held at a large, indoor arena. Competitors were milling around between the In and Out gates waiting for their turn. Each of us were between fifteen and nineteen, so I was one of the younger ones to qualify. When it was my turn, I made my run and exited the arena through the out gate. In front of God and everyone, including almost twenty of my peers, my mother pulled me off of my horse, took the bat [a small whip] from me, and proceeded to hit me with it while telling me that I had just made the worst run she'd ever seen.

I kept hoping I'd just die right there; instead, I slunk to the horse trailer where I cried my eyes out while unsaddling my horse. I hid under the bleachers to watch the remainder of the competition. When it was all said and done, I'd won first place. Again, I thought my mother would have to acknowledge that she was wrong and I had done a good job. Again, I was wrong. She told me I was lucky everyone else did terrible because it was still the worst run she'd seen. It was then that I realized I was never going to be "good enough" for her, so I decided to quit trying and told her to sell the horse.

That was the same year she divorced my dad, moving her new boyfriend in within a couple of months. He was a lot of fun, but he wasn't exactly "dad" material since he was only nine years older than me. Luckily, in spite of the divorce, my dad made sure to always be there for me, no matter what. He showed up even when she was too busy to bother. The FFA banquet when I was giving a speech? He was there over thirty minutes early, and she showed up over an hour after the entire event was over and cleaned up. He even sat there with me and waited for her. The school play when I had a lead role and was student director? Yep, he was early, and she missed the entire first act. Graduation? You guessed it; he arrived over an hour before the ceremony to tell me and my closest friends how proud he was of us; she skated in halfway through, which I would not have known except she told me, while laughing, in the reception line as she was telling me she had to leave for some other more pressing thing to do.

Meanwhile, her best friend was apologizing and giving me a gift. I had started looking to her when my mother was unavailable, and she was beginning to have a big influence on me. She showed the same unconditional love as my dad, and she looked out for me when my mother was too busy with herself. Of course, neither my father nor my stepmother showed up to any of these functions, so I guess I should be happy my mother came at all. It wasn't a conscious thought at the time, but I was learning that blood wasn't always thicker than water, and it definitely did not make a person family.

Let me back up a minute to tell you about my mother's third "motherly" moment. By high school, I hadn't gone for visitation at my father's for years. That was another pearl of wisdom from my mother—she never said a bad thing about Wayne that I can remember in spite of the abuse and lack of child support payments. What she did was let me figure out his character on my own. She suggested I wait for him to call me rather than me trying to call him. That call never came—he was my father, the same blood, a relative—yet he didn't care enough to pick up the phone for that call or to drive the ten miles to see me. I was maybe ten at the time I came to this realization.

Now, back to high school.... My senior year, my mother was deep into her "ME" years. I paid for enrollment in school, senior pictures, graduation announcements, cap and gown, gas for my pickup as well as the insurance on it, and a big chunk of my food by working two or three jobs during the afternoons, nights, and on weekends. Because I was working, my mother decided it was time for me to learn about being an adult and started charging me rent. I was dating and somewhat living with a 22–23-year-old, so my rent was basically to make sure I had a place to keep my clothes, a bed to sleep in every three or four nights and a shower when I did stay there. The day she woke me up at 6:00 a.m. to do "my chores," (dishes that weren't mine since I had been gone for a week), I decided it was time to move. At least my rent elsewhere would mean no 6:00 a.m. arguments over chores. Especially arguments that also involved her tossing ferrets under my sheets causing them to freak out and bite me until I got out of bed.

This led me to the first family of my choosing. I stayed with a friend at her parents' house until I figured out my next move. Her parents called me "kid," and I called them "Mom & Dad Good." They looked after me, made sure I never went hungry, and set down some basic ground rules. My clothes were tossed in amongst Nat's; we slept together in a queen bed when one or the other of us wasn't sleeping somewhere else; and I found unconditional love for the first time since my mother divorced my dad.

Next stop—Sisaboo and Daddy Frank. No blood, just mutual caring for one another. We were so close that I knew from 1000 miles away the night he was in a car wreck; I called her before she had time to get any information from the emergency room staff. They provided me with a home more than once over the next four years.

The first time I moved out of the Chance home, I got an apartment with my "sister" Vicki. She already had a little boy, so there were three of us in a one-bedroom. Let me just tell you, that was one crazy summer, but I learned a lot about what it means to truly be there for someone when the chips are down. Mostly because Vicki taught me... I was NOT a stellar roommate, but we had a system and a good time.

Vicki waited tables during the day, and I worked at a beer joint nights. She made sure I ate at least one decent meal a day through her job; I made sure she had beer through mine. It worked tremendously. We took care of her son together when he wasn't at his dad's house, and when he was, we made the most of it. I say "we" even though I am pretty sure I wasn't near as much help as I could have been since I was at a bar almost every night even when I wasn't working.

There were far too many escapades to recount, but I vividly remember the night we were at a party; she wasn't feeling very well and asked someone to come and get me. I found her leaning against the wheel of a car close to throwing up. Rather than actually taking care of her, I put her in her ex-boyfriend's car; I told her she'd be fine and went back to the party. We both made it to the apartment safely, albeit separately. The next morning, Vicki woke me up yelling about her car, which I had driven home. How I drove is unclear, but it definitely involved going through at least one barbed wire fence and a lot of meadow or ditches based on the scratches and grass we found. The battery was also dead because, apparently, I killed it and didn't bother to turn the key off. Not long after, she was driving my pickup and blew the motor. For a lot of people, these types of issues would have ended a friendship; for Vic and I, it just solidified our sisterhood.

By the end of summer, she was living with her boyfriend (who she would wind up marrying) and his two sons along with her son. Me? I went back to the Chances. I had decided to blow off a full academic scholarship in New Mexico because it was too far from home. My dad helped me go to a campus visit; it took almost twelve hours one way. Long distance phone calls were expensive and there wasn't any internet, which meant it wasn't going to be easy to stay in touch. I cried thinking about being so far from the one constant in my life—my dad. It was too much. I stayed in my rural hometown having a blast. I got a second job working at the soybean mill during harvest.

Sisaboo was dating a guy from a large extended family. The bean mill closed over the Thanksgiving holiday, so I wound up accompanying her to the guy's parents for the dinner. I've tried to emulate that day so many times! They welcomed me, some stray kid, as if I was their own. The people, the food, the games—all were endless, and it was the warmest feeling I'd known to that point in my life.

My mother manipulated the situation, and before I knew it, I was on a plane to Southern California to live with her dad and stepmother. During a conversation asking what I needed or wanted for Christmas, my mother told them I wanted a fresh start, that I was feeling lost after seeing my friends go off to college. As a result, I received a one-way plane ticket. If I thought the twelve hours to New Mexico were a long way from home, they were nothing compared to the almost twenty-four hours West Covina was. Fortunately, Gram and Gramps were not only family because of shared blood; they also cared enough to be there. Again, I was not a model housemate... I grew out of this; I promise. Ha-ha.

I snuck out of their house more times than I care to admit, but they never quit being there for me. Neither did my dad. After not quite two years, I decided to leave California and head home to Kansas. I didn't take into account the debts I had incurred would follow me. Dad came to my rescue and helped me work out payment plans for them. When I couldn't afford my truck payments, he helped me figure out how to return the pickup. Then, he helped pay my way BACK to California when I figured out I wasn't getting anywhere financially staying in Fredonia. Barely a year after that, I was back in Kansas. Again. Living with Kat and Frank. Again.

This time around, I was the one who started dating the guy with the big family. They weren't quite as welcoming, but they were very close-knit amongst themselves. The first time I spent the night with Joe, who would become my husband, it was a Saturday night. Before he took me back to Sis's, he said he needed to stop and tell his grandma what he was doing so she didn't worry. He parked on the street with about a dozen other vehicles, got out, looked at me, and said, "You coming?"

I was about to be initiated into Sunday Dinner. It was overwhelming—so many people, most of whom I did not know—made even more traumatizing when he introduced me to his Grandma Wanda as "Rosetta." I thought I was going to melt into the floor; then, I was devastated when I didn't. When his Grandpa Butch addressed the elephant in the room by asking Joe if he'd even bothered to ask my name before he got me undressed, I was mortified; twenty other people laughed. I survived that meal to attend many more.

Great-grandma Cummins, Grandma Wanda, [step] Grandpa Butch (with his hair piece), parents, aunts, uncles, cousins, siblings, babies, exes—one never knew who would be in attendance at Sunday Dinner, but you didn't miss it without a damned good reason. The menu, though, rarely changed: roast, fried chicken, potatoes and gravy were the core of every meal. After the dishes were cleared, washed, and dried, pitch or rummy or Rumikub were on the table. Arrive by 12:10, leave around 3:00. This went on for about six years until we moved out of town closer to my people.

Unfortunately, the sense of family had somewhat dissipated about a year before the move. It never returned, not even for my kids after Joe died. Their blood, their relatives, their "family" blamed me for Joe's death despite the fact that he was alone in the pickup, and it was a single-car accident. They reasoned that since our daughter looked too much like "that bitch" and our son looked too much like him, they just could stand to look at them, an eight- and nine-year-old.

Within a couple of years, I pulled the same method my mother used on me regarding my father; I told my kids to wait for their dad's family to reach out. It took almost a decade. Even then, it didn't last long. The yearly duty visit at Christmas is about the only time either of the kids see any of his family.

One thing about having moved closer to my people the year before Joe died was that they were there for us. I'd been able to reconnect with Vicki and Meredith, Natalie and Kathy, as well as develop a friendship with Nancy and Lorrie. These women became my rocks. A few others were added along the way, but these women? These women helped raise me and my kids for the first several years after Joe's death.

One of the reasons these women became my rocks is because Joe and I were pretty childish and dysfunctional the year before his death. We loved each other; we just didn't live together very well. In spite of this, in spite of not being willing to compromise, in spite of a divorce that left both of us in tears, in spite of months of anger and one-upping each other in the revenge game, he remained my best friend for the fourteen months we were apart before growing up, saying, "I'm sorry," and getting remarried.

One of the times we fought, Joe left and went to live with my mother. I remember saying something along the lines of "but you're my mother; you're supposed to take my side." Her response was to point out, "I like him better," again proving my belief that blood means nothing.

My friends, those nefarious women I mentioned, picked up the familial slack, so to speak. We said some pretty not nice things about my mother during those months. My children felt the bond among us and developed their own bonds with them. Even though I had siblings from additional marriages by both of my parents, my kids didn't know any of them. Instead, Hannah and Wyatt were on the ground floor of building our own functionally, dysfunctional amalgamation of people who would be our family no matter the time or space that sometimes happens.

Aunt Kathy. Aunt Vicki. Aunt Nat. Grandma and Grandpa Good. Aunt Nancy. Aunt Lorrie. Over the years, the ties that bind have been stretched, some have frayed, some were even broken and tied back together, never to be the same. But these are the ones who were there when my blood wasn't. These are the people who literally guarded my back and picked up my slack. Even now, if push comes to shove, any one of them would not hesitate to help out my kids. Kat lives in Alabama now. Nat works constantly. Mom Good passed away. Lorrie and I rarely speak anymore. But, if I asked, they'd be there for the kids.

Life and family both started to shift and look different a few months after Joe died. We moved to town, my hometown, and they became more active in recreational sports. They started having friends over or staying over with friends. A new family began to form. Another group of women, some without a spouse, some on husband or boyfriend number ???

In addition to the "aunts," Hannah and Wyatt soon gained a Momma Connie and a Momma Pam and a Momma Suzy while I became Momma Trish to a tribe consisting of their children. This tribe gave the kids brothers and sisters and cousins who continue to be family even as adults with their own children. Suffice it to say, our family is now extensive. Hopefully, none of the newest littles ever try to make a real family tree; they'll be so confused.

Don't mistake our family as being solely females. Shortly after Joe and I moved, a couple of years before his death, I met this guy at the manufacturing plant I worked in. I don't remember how or why, but he said something about my brother one day. I told him I didn't have any brothers. After telling me I needed one, he volunteered for the "job." He had actual brothers, three of them, and before any of us knew it, I had more brothers too. My kids gained a couple of uncles in the process.

Crazy, out of control, larger than life, dedicated uncles who have no blood ties to any of us. Two of the four are close to us; Uncle Troy, the original, is Brother and I am Sis. Uncle Todd is Bub and I am Sissy. The other two live elsewhere, so they aren't close to us, so I use their names. Once in a while, I do refer to the oldest as Brother Bear, though. Todd and Troy may not always make the best decisions in their lives, but they can always be counted on as brothers and uncles who will drop everything and help if it's within their power.

One time, when I couldn't reach anyone else to come help me with a flat tire on the side of the road, in the rain, Brother borrowed a car and a four-way and was on his way.

Ten miles isn't far, but when everyone has kids, jobs, and lives, it might as well be a thousand miles. We see one another intermittently, and at times, we don't even have the right phone number for each other, but they're family and I love them. I sat with the brothers and their children at their mom's funeral; even she understood and accepted that I was family.

It was in the middle of this new family that we acquired DJ. David Mark Hoover, Jr. to be exact. His dad and stepmother divorced, and she left with his four half siblings. DJ stayed with his dad until it became untenable. He was coming by my house after football practice a night or two a week, eventually coming every night. Within a couple of months, DJ was living with us and his name was on the chore calendar. Not long after, Hannah had a school assignment about who lived with her; she asked DJ if she could list him as her big brother. He tested my authority once by telling me he was going with friends and would be home later. When I asked if his chores were done, he told me I couldn't make him do dishes. I told him he was correct, but I could take the keys to the pickup away. He and his buddy did the dishes. Lesson learned. About a year after moving in, DJ was taken by his birth mother to Oklahoma.

She didn't like that we were close and forbid me and my kids from talking to DJ. It didn't take long for a system to be worked out in order to keep in touch. Upon his graduation two years later, he immediately started coming back to Kansas to spend time with us. We were introduced to two of his long-term girlfriends as his family. He called and asked us to come to Oklahoma to meet the second one, and to tell us they were having a baby. She commented that she was nervous about meeting and telling us because "we mattered." She had met his mother, but she said we were the ones whose opinions counted.

The day she went into labor, DJ called. Hannah and I took off for Oklahoma in less than an hour. Wyatt was deprived of this opportunity due to practice for the upcoming regional wrestling tournament. Ian was born shortly before we got to the hospital, but Hannah and I were one of the first people to hold him. Wyatt got the honor about a month later when we went to their house during spring break.

Sadly, shortly after that visit, DJ stopped calling and stopped answering our phone calls. He skipped Wyatt's senior prom and his graduation. I was able to reach Ashley shortly after Mother's Day, and she told me that DJ's biological mother was making an effort to be in his life, and he felt like he owed it to her to give her a chance, but he felt weird doing that while still talking to me. As a result, we lost David. This hurt my feelings, but it broke both of my kids' hearts. They rarely talk about him, and if he is mentioned, they just say "who?" Through his former stepmother, I know he is doing well and has more children.

Allow me to digress a little longer....

Momma Connie, my heart sister, has two sons and a daughter. Her two oldest, Dalton and Sunni, were in the same grade as Wyatt. Before long, it was impossible not to think of the five of them as siblings with all the covering for one another, the fighting with one another, and the sticking up for one another. Add in when the four oldest ganged up on poor little Walker—what a melee!!

Momma Pam (who is now Grammy Pammy) has several girls and a lone boy. Her youngest daughter, Christina, is Wyatt's age. Her son, Billy, is a year younger than them. Along with these ties, Wyatt had a fairly serious crush on one of the older daughters for a while when he was in fourth or fifth grade.

Momma Suzy had three boys, one of whom is Wyatt's age. Within a few years, we wound up living on the same block, and there were always extra boys in one house or the other.

With kids in sports, it is inevitable that games or practices are at the same time occasionally. One of these three ladies or Aunt Vicki could always be counted on to be at whichever game I wasn't. I am pretty sure that was when I realized it does take a village. Or a tribe. Or a large extended family. No one raises children or survives the stuff life throws at you in a bubble. You have to have those who hold you up when all you want to do is fall down.

As life tends to do, curve balls were thrown. Dating, divorces, marriages—we dealt with the highs and lows as they came, and we did it together. When Suzy died far too young and unexpectedly, Wyatt took several days, unpaid, off of work to come back home and be there for Bry. Pam and I held hands after the service and tried to make sense of it.

When Sunni was graduating from Fort Sill, Oklahoma, Hannah and I went with Connie for the family day. When Connie moved to Louisiana, we made a bunch of trips—one, two, or all three of us—to see her. At least once a month, even after a decade, I tell her to divorce her husband and move home so I can see her more often. Wyatt took a vacation to see Sunni in Hawaii where she is living since her husband is stationed there. Dalton and his wife brought their oldest from Texas to Kansas so we could meet him when he was a baby.

The larger, more geographically dispersed a family is, the more effort it takes to be there, but we do it when we can. Right down to two-hour phone calls in the middle of the night because the time difference makes it tough to do any other time of day. Right down to FaceTiming over three time zones to "see" one another for Easter.

Easter and Thanksgiving are my JAMS! Food and family are at the forefront of both, not to mention feeling blessed and thankful for another day together.

More than one holiday found us with another large family who took us in. Being a single parent made me take a look at who could take on the responsibility of my two children if something were to happen to me. The Mommas weren't options with so many of the kids being within one or two years of each other. The Aunts weren't options for a variety of reasons, not the least of which was that most of them were single and didn't need the added stress. As life will do, I found myself reconnecting with an acquaintance from childhood. She and her husband held similar values, and they agreed to take the kids on if necessary. They took their roles as "godparents" seriously, and we were invited to a number of their family functions, holidays, and even family reunions.

I wound up dating one of her nephews for a time—his brother's ex-wife, Steph, is still (nineteen years later) a part of our family. Her kids are my nephews and niece, and I'm their Aunt Trish. She's one of my sisters. She drove an hour to come and sit with me the night of the accident that took my parents. Because that's what family does. While in Oklahoma for the Women's College World Series this year, I noticed my "niece" MayMay and my grandson have the same dimples. I remarked that it proves we really are family.

Dating has brought me into contact with assorted family situations. While I am still friends with a couple of the men I've dated, their families didn't stick. Except one. Most likely because he and I had an off-and-on thing that started in high school and ended a couple of years ago because he's still in Fredonia with no plans to leave, and I don't really want to move back there again. Plus, my jobs have kept me away from Wilson County for several years, and we just couldn't make it work with me living elsewhere.

His family is amazing, and it breaks my heart a little that I'm not a full-fledged member. That isn't to say we aren't still close nor that any of them wouldn't move Heaven or Earth to help my kids or I. *** Slight update here.... We are no longer friends, not really. Due to a new girlfriend on his end, he skipped out on my mother's service even though he had asked about it, and told me several times, that he would be there. A lot of things are forgivable, but not this one, not this time.

Recently, I started dating someone completely out of my normal area. Freaking Tinder... smh.... He has an interesting mix of people in his world that make up his friends and family. He has been a rock through a LOT in a short time. My mother liked him; my dad never had the opportunity to meet him. The time we went to Dad's so I could introduce them was the day I put my dad in the hospital when we found him confused and inarticulate from a stroke.

Upon leaving the hospital, Dad went to a nursing home and wasn't allowed visitors due to the fear surrounding the coronavirus pandemic. When he returned home the week before Thanksgiving, things were terribly hectic. Since it was so close to the holiday, everyone thought that would be a good day to finally introduce the two men in my life. The car accident kept that from happening.

That day showed me that my children have also created their own family units. Several of their friends were also at my house for Thanksgiving dinner. Some of them stayed for hours to make sure Hannah and Wyatt were okay. When my kids and I, along with my Momma Susie and my full sister's daughter met at my mother's to make initial decisions, one of the spare kids came by to help with padlocks. His little boy walked into my mother's house and hollered for Grandma Bert. My heart broke at the same time it overflowed knowing that bond between him and my mother existed.

Another thing happened as a result of my dad's stroke and the accident. I gained a sister I'd had years ago but never had the opportunity to bond with. Dad had three daughters from his first marriage. His youngest, Andrea, is only about six months older than me but was a year ahead of me in school. Even though it was a small school, and we knew who each other were, we never bonded. We weren't even friends. The stroke changed that.

We pulled together to make the "right" decisions. We took turns at the hospital. We both stayed with him his first week home from the nursing home. During this time, we found out that we have a number of things in common, wrestlers for sons being one of them. Both of us were somewhat amazed that we missed all these opportunities to share our lives. Calling her was the most difficult thing to do after the accident. Yet again, we pulled together. We made more decisions trying to do what was right. I don't remember which of us said it first, but we both agreed that while God took our dad, he gave us a sister we didn't realize we needed. We text or call one another every couple of weeks just to check in. Her and her husband attended my mother's service even though they had to make an almost three-hour round trip to do so.

Easter 2021 was shaping up to be quite the affair. Three of my significant other's children were invited, as were his sister and some close friends of his who I've been lucky enough to bond with. Vicki and Mere (who is family in spite of her minimal acknowledgments in this manuscript). The godparents and Steph and all of their kids. Hannah and Wyatt and their "siblings" and children. A few other "kids" from along the way. Then there were two local family units who have repeatedly been there for me over the last four years. Had everyone who received an invite shown up, over fifty people would've broken bread together. Twenty-seven shared a meal, had quite a few laughs, and made some beautiful memories. It made things a little easier to get through the first family get-together since losing my parents.

Next up was the service for my mother. Since she was cremated, time wasn't an issue, so we were able to wait until the relatives from the West Coast could get to Kansas. This was another example, and further proof, that there are subtle differences between blood family and chosen family.

One of the uncles (you know, blood family) said, "If we can help, let us know." The other uncle said, "Do you need anything?" I told both of them I had everything covered, yet one of the uncles kicked in money to help pay for one of the meals, the other did not. The chosen family said, "We've got this" and helped with the meal after the service. The two local families gave me toilet paper, bottled water, and a few other essentials to help out while the relatives were at my house.

A couple of weeks before the memorial service for my mother, I was procrastinating homework for a grad class by binge watching old episodes of Grey's Anatomy while my significant other was out of town for work. Season Two, Episode Twelve originally aired on December 11,

2005, and as all episodes of the show do, it began and ended with a voiceover; this time it was Ellen Pompeo as Meredith Grey. Here is the part that hit me during this particular viewing:

"There's an old proverb that says you can't choose your family. You take what the fates hand you. And like them or not, love them or not, understand them or not, you cope. Then there's the school of thought that says the family you are born into is simply a starting point. They feed you, and clothe you, and take care of you until you're ready to go out into the world and find your tribe."

One thing that is funny, sort of, that the line says "they feed you, clothe you, and take care of you" as though these are the bare minimum basics of what a family does. The reason it's funny is because a guy from my church was in school with, and friends with, my mother's oldest brother, and on Mother's Day one year, he told me he was proud of the mom I was based on the example, or lack thereof, I had in my own mother. By his estimation, my mother thought being a parent was the equivalent of a wolf—"I provided food and shelter; what more do you need?" I made a halfhearted attempt to defend her, but we both knew he had summed up my childhood quite well. That said, I guess she did a decent job since I survived long enough to find my tribe.

I think Meredith Grey, or the writers of Grey's Anatomy more specifically, only had it partially right, though, back in 2005, and if asked in 2021, she'd agree with me.

Here's my clarification, or extension, of that 2005 observation: as we grow, we change, and as we change, so does our tribe. Some people remain regardless; however, some pass through quickly while others fade away slowly. Some are replaced, and others serve their purpose and don't need anyone to fill their spot when they leave the family. And sometimes, any and all can reappear to get you through or set you straight.

Lessons my mother taught me:
1. If you fall off the horse, you have to get back on.
2. Learn to cook.
3. Take care of the animals.
4. Make time for the hard conversations.
5. The first time isn't all it's cracked up to be.
6. Fess up, no matter what.

Lessons my father taught me:
1. Know the difference between punishment and abuse.
2. Fear is a powerful tool. Or a weapon.
3. Even good people have a breaking point.
4. Know your limits.
5. Skeletons aren't as hidden as you think even if no one talks about them.
6. Forgiveness may take years, but it is possible.

Lessons my Momma Susie taught me:
1. A fresh manicure cures a lot of ills.
2. Buy the dress, and make time to wear it.
3. Find a signature perfume.
4. Accessorize.
5. Have a backup plan and a Go Bag.
6. Always have an alibi.

Lessons my dad taught me:
1. Never gamble more than you can afford to lose.
2. Listen.
3. Give people grace, especially if they can't give it to themselves.

4. Save your money, but don't forget you can't take it with you.
5. Learn as many new skills as you can.
6. Love with all that you have.

Lessons my late husband taught me:
1. Staying mad is a waste of time.
2. Take the vacation.
3. Live. Every single day.
4. Sometimes, silence speaks volumes.

Lessons my full sister taught me:
1. Sometimes, you gotta cut your losses.
2. Nurture over nature.

Lessons my half-sister taught me:
1. Sometimes you find refuge from the storm in the most random places.
2. You can do anything, but you have to try.

Lessons my stepsister taught me:
1. It really is never too late.
2. Be there for one another.
3. The Lord will provide.

Lessons my heart-siblings taught me:
1. Neither time nor distance matter.
2. Make time for one another.
3. Everyone needs a brother.

Lessons my maternal grandmother taught me:
1. Keep dancing.
2. Host the holiday meal.
3. Save the good stories for the great-grandchildren.

Lessons my paternal grandmother taught me:
1. Words have meaning.
2. Stand firm in your beliefs.
3. Memories make beautiful quilts.

Lessons my maternal grandfather taught me:
1. Learn military time.
2. Marry someone who gets you—warts and all—and loves you anyway.
3. A car warms up just as fast with you driving it as it does idling in the driveway.

Lessons my paternal grandfather taught me:
1. Eat dessert first.
2. Baseball is a beautiful thing.
3. Black coffee puts hair on your chest.